S0-AIP-725

DISCARDED
by the
Chelmsford Public Library
Chelmsford, MA

Published by Creative Education
123 South Broad Street, Mankato, Minnesota 56001
Creative Education is an imprint of The Creative Company

Design and production by Stephanie Blumenthal
Printed in the United States of America

Photographs by Galyn C. Hammond, The Image Finders (Mark Gibson, Werner Lobert, William Manning), JLM Visu-
als (Richard P. Jacobs, Breck P. Kent, Craig Kesselheim, John Minnich), Robert McCaw, Tom Myers, James P. Rowan,
Eugene G. Schulz, Tom Stack & Associates (Erwin & Peggy Bauer, Tommy Dodson, Terry Donnelly, Jeff Foott, Robert
Fried, Lynn Geri, Sharon Gerig, Joe McDonald, Peter Mead, Milton Rand, Doug Sokell, Dave Watts, Jim Yokajty)

Copyright © 2007 Creative Education
International copyright reserved in all countries. No part of this book may be reproduced in any form
without written permission from the publisher.

Library of Congress Cataloging-in-Publication Data

Bodden, Valerie.
Deserts / by Valerie Bodden.
p. cm. — (Our world)
Includes index.
ISBN-13 : 978-1-58341-461-3
1. Deserts—Juvenile literature. I. Title. II. Series.
QH88.B63 2006   578.754—dc22   2005053717

First Edition
2 4 6 8 9 7 5 3 1

MCC

Direct
1-29-07
24 25
JNF
578.
754
BODD

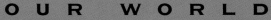

O U R   W O R L D

Chelmsford Public Library
Children's Dept.
Chelmsford, MA 01824

D E S E R T S

Valerie Bodden

Deserts are dry, sandy places. They are found all over the world. Some deserts are very big. The biggest desert in the world is called the Sahara (Suh-HARE-uh) Desert. It is in Africa. The Sahara Desert is bigger than the United States!

The sun shines a lot in deserts. It makes deserts very hot during the day. Deserts are hot during the day all year long. They are even hot in the winter! At night, the sun goes down. Then deserts get cold.

Most deserts are hot and sandy places

It does not rain much in deserts. Sometimes deserts do not get any rain for a whole year! There are not many lakes in deserts. There are not many rivers, either.

*The hot sun dries up
the ground in deserts*

The ground in deserts is covered with sand. Some-times the sand blows around. It makes **sand dunes**. Some of the sand dunes are very high!

The wind piles desert sand into dunes

There are lots of rocks in some deserts. Some of the rocks are small. Others are huge. Some deserts even have **mountains**.

The rocks in deserts are all different shapes

Flowers cover the ground in some deserts

Not many plants grow in deserts. There is not enough rain for most plants. But a few plants grow in deserts. The **cactus** is a plant. It grows in some deserts. Flowers can grow in deserts, too. Many flowers are yellow. Others are orange or red.

Lots of animals live in deserts. Camels live in some deserts. So do mice. **Coyotes** (ky-OH-tees) live in some deserts, too.

Many desert animals have light-colored fur

Lizards, birds, and bugs all live in deserts

All kinds of snakes live in deserts. Lizards live there. So do birds. Lots of spiders and **insects** live in deserts, too.

Animals that live in deserts try not to get too hot. Most animals in deserts come out at night. It is not hot then. Snakes move around at night. Spiders run across the ground. Coyotes hunt for food. Nighttime is a busy time in a desert!

Deserts seem empty but are often full of life

Should you wear white or black clothes to stay cool in a desert? Here is a way to find out. Put two thermometers in the sun. Cover one with a white cloth. Cover the other one with a black cloth. Have a grown-up help you check the thermometers in half an hour. Which one is hotter?

GLOSSARY

cactus—a plant that has spines, or thorns, and grows in deserts

coyotes—gray animals that look like dogs

insects—bugs that have six legs

mountains—very big hills

sand dunes—big hills of sand

LEARN MORE ABOUT DESERTS

Arizona-Sonora Desert Museum
http://www.desertmuseum.org/kids

Desert Sandbox Kids' Page
http://www.dpcinc.org/kids_pics.htm

Living Desert Coloring Pages
http://www.livingdesert.org/pdf/coloringpages.pdf

INDEX